THE COMMON COLD

THE COMMON COLD

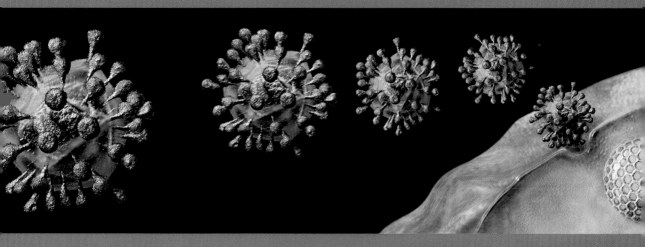

Terry Allan Hicks

 **Marshall Cavendish**
Benchmark
New York

With thanks to Renato N. Mascardo, M.D., FACE, FACP, Assistant Clinical Professor of Medicine, Division of Endocrinology & Metabolism, University of Connecticut School of Medicine, for his expert review of the manuscript.

Marshall Cavendish Benchmark
99 White Plains Road
Tarrytown, New York 10591-9001
www.marshallcavendish.us

Library of Congress Cataloging-in-Publication Data

Hicks, Terry Allan.
   The common cold / by Terry Allan Hicks.
      p. cm. — (Health alert)
   Summary: "Discusses the common cold and its effects on people and society"—Provided by publisher.
   Includes index.
   ISBN 0-7614-1913-6
   1. Cold (Disease)—Juvenile literature. I. Title. II. Series: Health alert (Benchmark Books)

   RF361.H53 2005
   616.2'05--dc22   2005004999

Front cover: Cold viruses
Title page: Cold viruses

The photographs in this book are used by permission and through the courtesy of:

Front cover: Dr. Linda Stannard, UCT / Photo Researchers, Inc.
Photo Researchers, Inc.: Russell Kightley, 2, 16; Dr. Linda Stannard, UCT, 5, 14, 15; Dr. S. Patterson, 13; Kent Wood, 17; Eye of Science, 19; Nibsc, 21; A.B. Dowsett, 23; John Bavosi, 24; Mark Clarke, 25; Science Photo Library, 31; National Library of Medicine, 34; Geoff Bryant, 40 (left); Will & Deni McIntyre, 40 (right); NCI, 41; Erich Schrempp, 49; TH FOTO-WERBUNG, 51; Stephanie Boulay, 52; Laurent / Caroline, 55; Oscar Burriel, 56. *HIP/Scala / Art Resource, NY:* 27. *Corbis:* Hulton-Deutsch Collection, 29; Bettmann, 32, 33, 35, 39; Dick Clintsman, 44; Jose Luis Pelaez, Inc., 53. *Superstock:* 11. *Getty:* Britt Erlanson / Image Bank, 12; Hulton Archive, 37; Peter Cade, 43, 47; Ghislain & Marie David de Lossy, 48; 3D Clinic, 54. *Terry Allan Hicks:* 8.

Printed in China

6 5 4 3 2 1

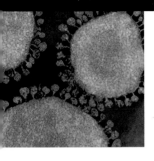

CONTENTS

Chapter 1   What Is It Like to Have a Cold?   6

Chapter 2   What Is the Common Cold?   10

Chapter 3   The History of the Common Cold   26

Chapter 4   Coping with the Common Cold   42

Glossary   58

Find Out More   61

Index   63

WHAT IS IT LIKE TO HAVE A COLD?

Jamie, a five-year-old boy, is lying on the living room couch, covered with a blanket and feeling awful. Not even watching his favorite television shows is making him feel better. He is sick with a cold. (A cold is sometimes called the common cold.)

It all started about two days ago. Jamie's throat felt sore and a bit "scratchy," and his voice sounded rough and hoarse when he talked. He began complaining of a headache, and his mother noticed that his face was red, or flushed. His mother took his temperature with a thermometer and discovered that he had a fever. Jamie's fever was not very high—only a little higher than the usual body temperature of 98.6 degrees Fahrenheit. His mother gave him some medication that made the fever go away for a while. But Jamie's fever returned several times over the past two days.

Jamie also has other **symptoms**—or signs—of a cold. A thin, watery substance called **mucus** started to drip out of his nose. He was also coughing up mucus. Over the last two days, the mucus became thick and slimy, and there was a lot more of it. This thick substance called **phlegm**, is blocking his **airways,** making it difficult for him to breathe. When he coughs, he can feel mucus—he calls it "gunk"—coming up out of his throat and into his mouth. And when he sneezes, even more mucus comes out of his nose. This build-up of mucus in his airways is called **congestion.** It affects Jamie's sense of smell, and taste. Even his favorite foods "just don't taste right," he says.

While he has a cold, Jamie suffers from **fatigue,** which means he feels very tired all the time. His fever eventually goes away, but now he has the opposite feeling: chills. He is shivering and trembling as if the room were freezing cold, even though he is wearing warm clothes and is covered with a blanket. But for Jamie, the worst part of this cold is a hard-to-describe feeling of not being well. As he puts it, "I just feel really bad, and I can't even explain why." Doctors call this symptom **malaise.**

While he has this cold, Jamie has been staying home from school. This is partly to make sure he has time to get well. But it is also because Jamie might be **contagious.** This means that other people who come in contact with him could "catch" his cold. By staying home until he feels better, he is

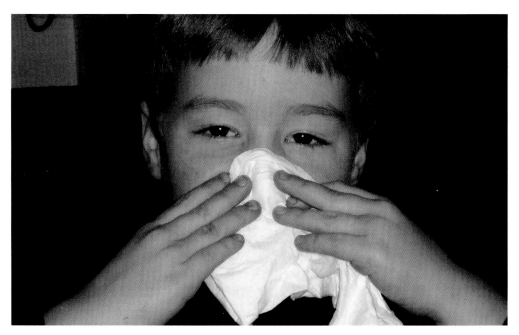

Jamie is used to having colds. He knows this one will mean about a week of coughing, sneezing, and feeling tired and miserable.

helping to keep the other children at his school healthy. But he must be careful at home, too, because he has a baby brother—and he knows babies can easily catch colds like his. So even though he loves to play with baby Andrew, he knows he has to keep away from him until his cold is gone.

If Jamie's cold symptoms get much worse, or if they seem to be lasting longer than usual, he will probably have to see his doctor. This is partly because he has a serious medical condition, called **asthma,** that sometimes makes it difficult for him to breathe. Having a cold can make his asthma worse, and Jamie's doctor might want to give him some medication to protect against this.

Some medication may be given when a person has a cold. A few times since Jamie's cold began, his mother has given him acetaminophen. It helped take away his fever and headache for a while. But even if Jamie does take more medication, it will not make his cold go away. Different kinds of medication can help with some cold symptoms, such as fever, headaches, coughing, sneezing, and sore throat. To help him feel better, Jamie's mother is making sure that he gets plenty of rest, drinks lots of orange juice and water, eats a lot of chicken soup, and stays warm. But there is no cure for the common cold itself—except time.

Within a day or two, Jamie will probably be well enough to return to school. His fever and headaches will be gone, and he will be coughing and sneezing much less than he is now. At first, he may not have quite as much energy as he usually does, so he may not be able to run around on the playground for a few more days. But he will soon be him-self again and can go back to being an active five-year-old.

2

WHAT IS THE COMMON COLD?

The common cold really is very common. In fact, it is probably the most common illness in the world. In the United States alone, experts estimate that there are at least half a billion colds—and possibly twice that many—in a typical year.

The common cold is an **infection** caused by a **microorganism** that enters the body from outside. This microorganism, called a **virus,** attacks the upper **respiratory system,** which carries air to the lungs. The basic symptoms of the common cold include coughing, sneezing, sore throat, congestion, fatigue, and malaise. Someone who has a cold may also suffer from headaches, body aches, chills, and fever. These symptoms are often very unpleasant, but for most people the common cold is not a very serious illness. Most colds will end in three to seven days, whether they are treated or not. In some cases, however, colds can make existing medical conditions, such as asthma, worse. A cold can also lead to more serious illnesses, including **pneumonia, bronchitis,** and influenza.

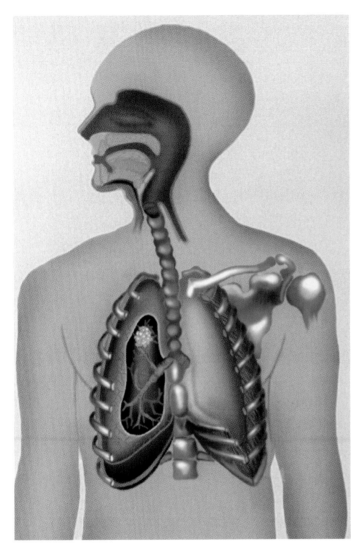

The respiratory system carries air—and microorganisms such as viruses—into the human body.

Doctors and scientists have been studying the common cold for many years. Yet there are many things about colds that they still do not understand. For example, why do some people catch colds more often than others?

Children usually have more colds than adults. Studies show that a child catches about six to ten colds a year. Babies are even more likely to have colds than older children. A baby may have nine or more colds in its first year of life.

One reason is that children have not yet had time to develop **immunity** to certain infections. Immunity is the body's ability to prevent and fight illness or diseases. Usually, a person's immune system—the body system responsible for fighting infection—becomes

The younger you are, the more likely it is that you will catch a cold.

more developed and stronger as he or she grows. Another reason children catch many colds may have to do with coming in contact with other children with colds. Children who are contagious can be found at school, in day care centers, or on the playground. Some researchers believe that at any time, one out of four children in a day care center may have a cold.

Most adults usually have only about two to four colds a year. Women are more likely to catch colds than men, especially when they are between the ages of twenty and thirty. This may be because, at this age, they are often caring for children who are contagious. As they get older, both men and women catch fewer colds. After the age of sixty, most people have only about one cold in a year. However, if an adult is sick with an illness or disease that affects the immune system, he or she may catch more colds than a healthy adult.

The common cold is one of the toughest problems facing

medical science. Far more serious diseases can now be prevented or cured. But there is no medication that keeps people from getting colds, and there is no cure for people who already have colds. But we do know much more about colds than we did in the past. Most importantly, we know what causes the common cold.

WHAT IS THE COLD VIRUS?

Viruses are very mysterious things, and the scientists who study them still do not completely understand them. One reason is that they are incredibly small. They are among the smallest of all living things. Viruses are too small to see without using a very strong microscope. Most viruses are only about 1/100,000 of an

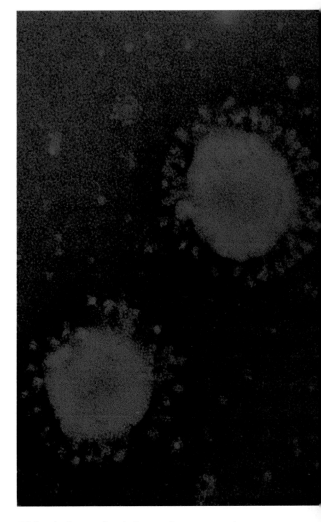

This photograph—taken using a very strong microscope called an electron microscope—shows two cold viruses.

inch long, and some are just one-billionth of an inch in length. Some experts believe that about 300 billion viruses could fit on the period at the end of this sentence.

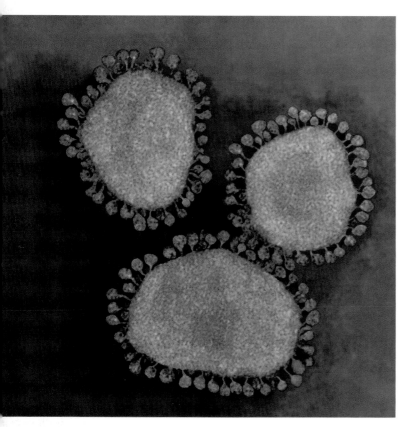

A coronavirus—a type of cold virus—takes it name from its outer layer. The layer is called a "corona," (meaning "crown") that it uses to attach itself to a host cell.

Unlike other organisms, viruses cannot breathe, eat, or grow. The only quality they share with other organisms—the only thing that makes them truly "alive"—is that they can reproduce. Reproduction is the process involved in creating the offspring of living things. For example, human offspring are called babies and children. For some organisms, reproduction involves creating copies of an organism. Viruses reproduce by making copies of themselves. But they cannot do that without the help of another organism.

A virus is a **parasite.** This means it needs another organism, called a **host**, in order to reproduce and survive for long periods of time. Some viruses can exist without a host, but not for very long. The process by which a virus uses a host is very complex. Put simply, viruses invade hosts' cells—the small basic units of living things. A virus attaches itself to the outer layer

Different Kinds of Colds

The cold viruses belong to several different "families," including the rhinovirus, coronavirus, and respiratory syncytial virus (RSV) groups. These groups are determined based on the way the virus is shaped and how it behaves and affects the host. Rhinoviruses are the leading cause of the common cold. They are responsible for at least 30 percent of all colds. Coronaviruses are the second most-common cause of colds.

Different cold viruses behave differently. The colds caused by coronaviruses, for example, are usually fairly mild in adults, but they can be quite serious for young children. And rhinoviruses affect people mostly during the spring, summer, fall, and winter, while coronaviruses tend to cause winter colds. With both types of cold virus, a sick person can experience congestion, fever, coughing, sore throat, and malaise.

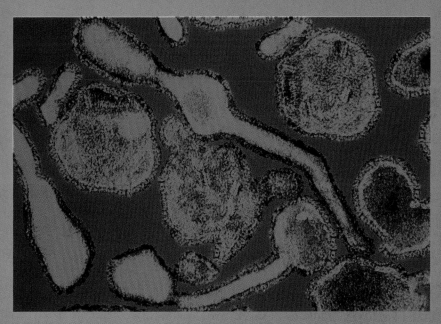

Respiratory syncytial viruses, like the ones shown here, cause infections that are especially serious for young children.

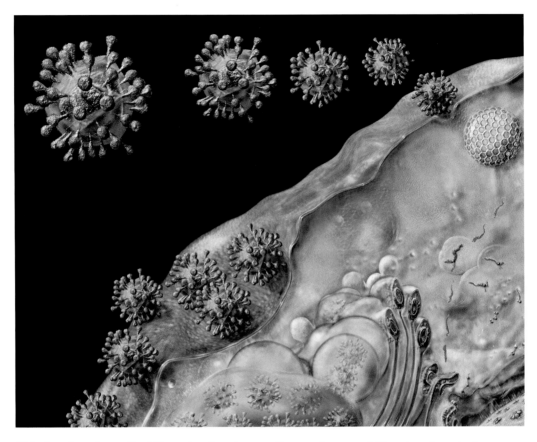

This drawing shows the life cycle of a virus as it reproduces and then bursts out of a host cell.

of the host cell, and then bores through it. It then takes over the host cell and uses the cell's energy and matter to reproduce copies of the virus. The copies then burst from the host cell to escape, killing the host cell. This process is not always deadly to the host organism, but it often causes serious damage. This is because in most cases, many copies of the virus are attacking multiple host cells at the same time. Often the host organism is able to kill the virus and replace the lost cells. But this depends on the type of virus. Different viruses cause many diseases in humans, including some types of cancer, acquired immune deficiency syndrome (AIDS), smallpox, influenza, and, of course, the common cold. Scientists have identified about two hundred different viruses that cause the common cold.

Being affected by a cold begins with exposure. This occurs when a person comes in contact with the cold virus, which can happen in many ways. A person can inhale or breathe in the virus, along with tiny droplets of moisture sprayed into the air by a sick person who has sneezed or coughed. (Research suggests that these droplets can hang in the air for as long as thirty minutes.) Most researchers now believe, however, that the most common way for the cold virus to be passed on is by touch.

A sneeze can send mucus flying through the air at more than 100 miles per hour.

Suppose someone in your family, or in your class at school, has a cold. That person might touch something—a doorknob, for example—with a hand that has already been used to wipe a

The Cold Season

People can catch the common cold throughout the whole year. But there is a definite "cold season," when people are far more likely to become ill. In North America, the cold season usually begins in late August or early September, and does not end until March or April.

Why these months? One theory is that at this time of year it is usually quite cool, and people are spending more time indoors. Once inside, they come in closer contact with people—some of whom might be infected with cold viruses. But there may be other reasons. Most of the viruses that cause the common cold survive better in dry conditions, and the air is usually drier in the winter than at other times of the year. Because of this, people's nasal membranes—tissues that line the nose—are also drier, which makes it easier for the viruses to live in them.

runny nose. If you touch the doorknob, then brush your hand over your face, the virus can enter your body through your nose or mouth. And you may soon be infected with a cold virus, too.

THE BODY DEFENDS ITSELF

The human body's first line of defense against the cold virus—and other illnesses—begins with physical barriers that block viruses and other foreign matter, such as dust, dirt, or **germs.**

Your nose is lined with little hairs that keep foreign matter—such as water droplets carrying viruses and other microorganisms—from entering the body. The skin inside the nose is covered with a thin coating of mucus that can trap viruses. The warmth and wetness inside the nose also help fight cold viruses, which usually survive best in cool, dry conditions. These defenses are very effective, but many viruses still reach the back of the nose and enter the throat. There are barriers in the throat, too—another layer of mucus, and many **cilia** (tiny hairlike projections), which can also trap viruses. Mucus, dirt, dust, and germs caught in the throat are expelled— pushed out—through coughing that occurs naturally throughout the day.

Cilia (shown here 2,000 times their actual size) help trap foreign matter entering the respiratory system.

But when the virus gets past these physical barriers, the body becomes infected. The human body has a complex and powerful defense system against disease and illness. It is known as the immune system. The immune system's defenses begin working once the body realizes it has been infected.

Antibodies are produced by **white blood cells** to fight off the viruses. Antibodies are special proteins that attack body invaders—like a virus. The antibodies that are created to fight off a virus attack are called **immunoglobulins.** These antibodies are very effective virus-fighters, because they prevent the virus from attaching itself to a healthy host cell.

The immune system also has other lines of defense. When healthy cells become aware that they are under attack by a virus, they begin producing chemicals called **prostaglandins.** This process can usually feel unpleasant, because prostaglandins make the affected areas swollen and painful. (This is one of the causes of congestion, especially in the nose.)

The presence of prostaglandins also attracts a special type of white blood cell, called **neutrophils,** to the infected area. The neutrophils actually "eat" some of the viruses, helping to stop the attack—but they also cause more swelling. This swelling, or inflammation, can make the person who has a cold feel awful. But it is necessary to help fight off the infection. Swollen tissue has a higher temperature, which makes it more difficult for the cold virus to reproduce.

Another substance produced by infected cells is called **histamine.** This substance makes the body—especially the

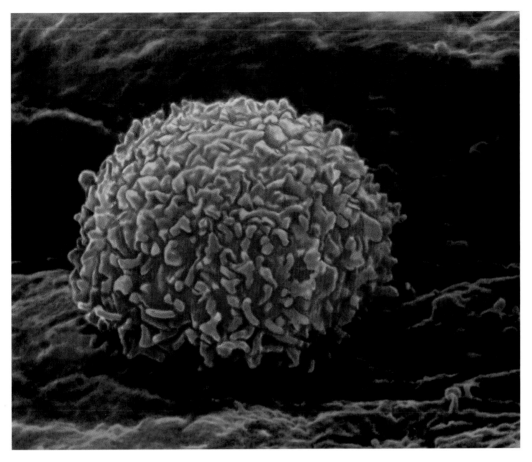

Neutrophils are white blood cells that fight infection by destroying foreign particles such as viruses.

nose—produce more mucus to trap virus cells. But it also causes some of the most irritating cold symptoms, including sore throat, muscles aches, and watery discharge from the nose.

These defenses will sometimes stop a cold by themselves. If they do not, the immune system begins producing even more powerful white blood cells, called **monocytes** and **lymphocytes.** Monocytes turn into a special kind of cell that can "eat" as many as one hundred virus cells. Some lymphocytes are even more powerful. Different ones prevent virus cells from reproducing, while others create infection-fighting chemicals within the body. **Interleukin** is one of these chemicals. One of its effects is to raise the temperature in the infected area. This slows down virus reproduction, but also causes fever and aches.

Some types of lymphocytes also produce chemical defenses called **interferons.** Scientists do not yet completely understand how interferons work, but they know that in some way they keep already-infected cells from reproducing.

If a viral attack succeeds in making its way past all these defenses, the viruses attach themselves to the cells and force these host cells to make copies of the virus cells. The virus attack spreads with incredible speed. Within just twelve hours, between 900,000 and one million cells in the cold victim's nose and throat may have been invaded by viruses. After twenty-four hours, the attacked cells may have created as many as 90 million viruses. And every one of them is hard at work creating even more.

The body tries to remove the dead cells in the nose and throat, by producing thin, watery mucus from the nose. You probably know this as one of the first signs that you are getting a cold—a runny nose. The buildup of dead cells in the throat also causes a sore or "scratchy" throat. These are just some of the many symptoms that are caused not by the illness itself, but by the body's attempts to fight it.

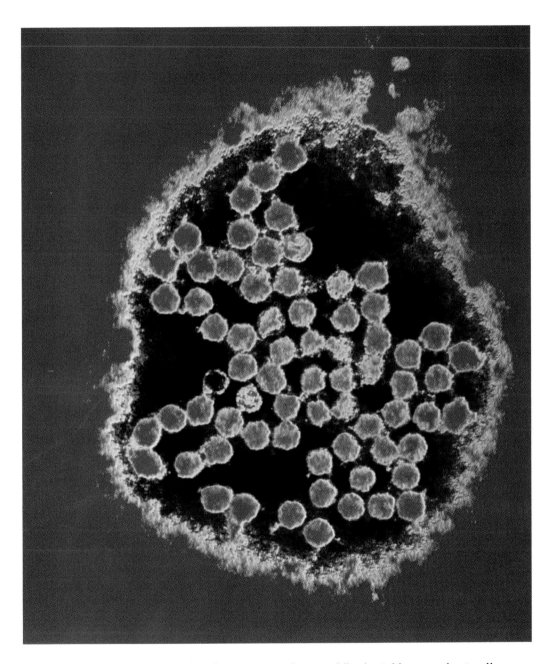

Viruses—like this group of rhinoviruses—reproduce rapidly, by taking over host cells.

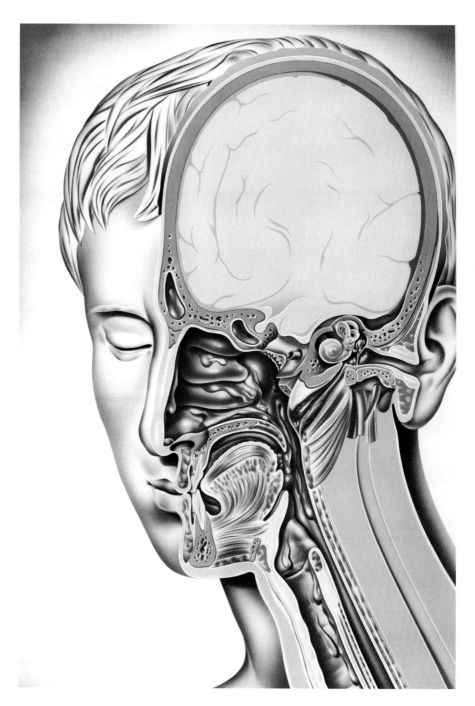

When you have a cold, mucus (the yellow fluid shown here) drips down your nose and throat.

Coughing and sneezing can also indicate that you have a cold. By coughing, you are forcing mucus—which is loaded with infected cells—out of your throat. Sneezing, too, helps to remove the cold virus from your body, though it is not nearly as effective as coughing.

After a few days, your body will most likely defeat the cold virus. The cold symptoms will slowly begin to disappear. If you had a fever, your temperature will drop back to normal. The coughing, sneezing, headaches, body aches, and general malaise will eventually fade away.

When Are You Contagious?

....

It is very difficult to tell when you are most likely to infect others with the cold virus. This is because the **incubation period**—the time it takes for the viruses to multiply and affect you—for a cold begins about two days before any symptoms appear. The incubation period may last as long as five days after the symptoms appear. Doctors generally agree that you are *most* contagious when you have early cold symptoms: coughing, sneezing, and a runny nose. As the illness progresses, your contagiousness usually lessens.

Coughing helps you fight off a cold, by forcing infected mucus out of your body.

3

THE HISTORY OF THE COMMON COLD

People have been suffering from colds—and trying to find ways to cure them and ease their symptoms—for as long as anyone can remember.

Three thousand years ago, the Chinese treated colds with a tea brewed from the *ma huang* plant. This plant produces a chemical called ephedrine. Today, certain forms of ephedrine are used in medication to reduce sinus congestion and other cold symptoms.

The famous early Greek physician Hippocrates—who lived around 460 B.C.E. to 377 B.C.E.—believed colds occurred when "waste matter" built up in the brain. When this waste matter overflowed, it caused runny noses. This is why the Greeks called the common cold *catarrh,* meaning "flow." *Catarrh* is still a word we use in English today.

Other doctors in ancient Greece thought they could release the waste matter in the body by bloodletting—allowing the patient's blood to flow. They did this either by simply cutting the skin or by placing leeches—small bloodsucking animals— on the patient's skin.

Some of the ancient "cures" for the common cold were even stranger. Pliny the Elder, a Roman scientist who lived in the first century C.E., thought that kissing a mouse's nose would help someone stop sneezing and coughing. These long-ago cold remedies were not helpful, and some of them probably made the patient feel even worse. But the doctors of the past were not always wrong. Maimonides, a Jewish scholar who lived from 1135 C.E. to 1204 C.E., recommended that people suffering from colds drink chicken soup. Hundreds of years later, medical research showed that this was very good advice.

Have you ever wondered why people sometimes say, "Bless you!" when someone sneezes? This began hundreds of years ago, in Europe, during the Middle Ages. It was believed

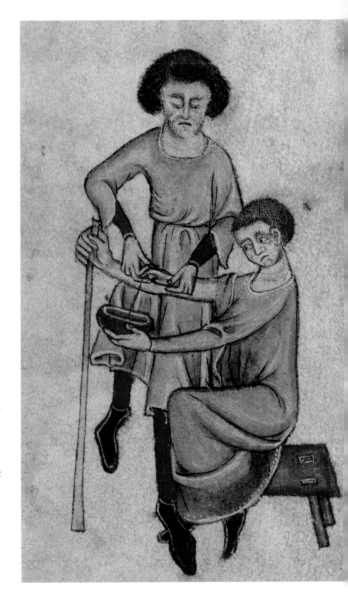

This painting from the Middle Ages shows a doctor treating a patient by "bleeding" him—cutting open a blood vessel. In the past, many doctors believed that this form of treatment would cure many different illnesses.

that illnesses such as colds were caused by evil spirits in the body. People feared that if they sneezed, their souls would leave their bodies. When someone sneezed, they would say a prayer—"God bless you!"—to keep this from happening. We still do this today, though most of us have no idea why.

People in the Middle Ages (which was from around 400 C.E. to 1400 C.E.) tried many other cures for the common cold. One of the smelliest might have been the habit of wearing necklaces made of garlic or salted fish. Though they did not cure people's colds, the necklaces most likely helped to prevent the spread of the illness. Most people would not want to get near or touch someone who wore such smelly necklaces.

THE COMMON COLD IN MODERN TIMES

Beginning in the eighteenth century, doctors began to take a more scientific approach to understanding the common cold. Their studies showed that many of the things people believed about colds were simply not true. For example, they proved that colds were not caused by miasmas, which were poisonous gases believed to be released by the earth.

One theory about cold-catching still circulates today. For centuries, people have thought that being exposed to cold temperatures caused colds. (In fact, this belief is probably how the common cold got its name.) One person who did not believe this was Benjamin Franklin, who was one of America's Founding Fathers. He was not a doctor, but he was a scientist.

He made a very good guess about what caused colds. They came, he said, from "animal Substances in perspired Matter from our Bodies, passed by the Air. People catch Colds when . . . near each other so as to breathe each other's Transpiration."

Franklin was not alone in believing that colds were caused by what we now call microorganisms. By his time, scientists already knew that **bacteria** and other tiny organisms existed. The first person to actually see bacteria was probably Antony van Leeuwenhoek, a Dutch scientist and lensmaker who was one of the creators of the early microscope. In 1683, he published detailed descriptions of bacteria that he had observed through a microscope he had built.

It was another two centuries before researchers began to understand the link

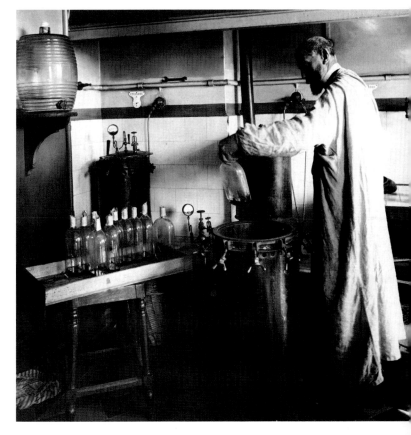

Chemist Louis Pasteur made many important scientific discoveries in his laboratory in Paris.

between microorganisms and disease. In the 1860s, a French chemist named Louis Pasteur proposed what he called the germ theory, which proposed that many diseases were caused by microorganisms, such as bacteria. This was a very controversial idea, and many of Pasteur's fellow scientists refused to believe it at first. But the germ theory laid the groundwork for much of the research into disease in the century and a half since then.

Viruses were first discovered in 1898, by a Dutch botanist named Martinus Beijerinck, who was studying a disease in tobacco plants. He used a very fine filter to remove all bacteria from the plants, but found that the disease was still present. This seemed to show that something even smaller than bacteria—something too small to be seen with a microscope— was causing the disease. Even though Beijerinck could not see it, he was sure it existed. He called it a virus. The name actually means "poison" or "slime" in Latin.

These researchers were increasing the real scientific knowledge about diseases such as the common cold. But at the same time, more and more sick people were taking untested, and sometimes dangerous medicine for their illnesses. These were called patent medicine and were usually not prescribed by real doctors. The patent medicine was sold on street corners or in medicine shows. These shows were like traveling carnivals that used entertainment to attract people who might buy the medicines.

Martinus Beijerinck, a scientist in the Netherlands, discovered viruses—even though they were too small to see with the microscopes of the time.

A man sells patent medicines on the streets of London, England, in 1876.

The medicines were packaged in fancy bottles, and given colorful names such as Dr. Bonker's Celebrated Egyptian Oil and White Eagle Rattle-Snake Oil. Their labels made claims that were almost certainly untrue. Hicks' Capudine Cure, for example, was supposed to be able to cure "headaches . . . colds, la grippe [influenza] and catarrh." Many patent medicines were supposed to be effective treatments for diseases—such as cancer—that doctors cannot completely cure even today.

Most of these patent medicines were of very little value against disease. Many were little more than colored water flavored with herbs, and often a large amount of alcohol. Some of them were probably quite dangerous. One problem was that they might make people think they did not need to see a doctor, which could make their medical problems worse. But some of these "cures"

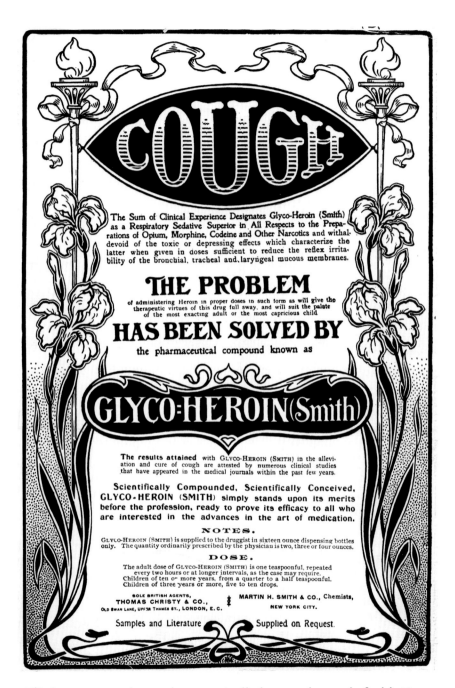

This long-ago cough remedy may actually have made people feel better, but its main ingredient—heroin—is an extremely dangerous habit-forming drug.

This nineteenth-century illustration shows a woman bringing hot soup, medicine, and a warm blanket to someone who has a cold.

actually contained very dangerous drugs. Some—like the so-called Taylor Cherokee Remedy—contained dangerous, habit-forming drugs, such as cocaine, heroin, and morphine. The dangers of these patent medicines led the United States government to closely regulate—or control—such medicines, early in the twentieth century.

One medicine that actually proved quite helpful had been available since the mid-1900s. For centuries, people had brewed a tea from the bark of the willow tree to stop pain and reduce fever. In the 1830s, a German drug company, Bayer, identified the active ingredient in the bark, called salicylic acid, and began producing a drug called acetylsalicylic acid. We know it today as aspirin. Scientists today, however, do not advise taking aspirin for colds.

THE 1900s AND BEYOND

By the early 1900s, scientists were beginning to have a deeper understanding of what caused colds. A German scientist named Walter von Kruse conducted an experiment that proved that something other than bacteria must cause the common cold. He took samples of mucus from the noses of people who had colds,

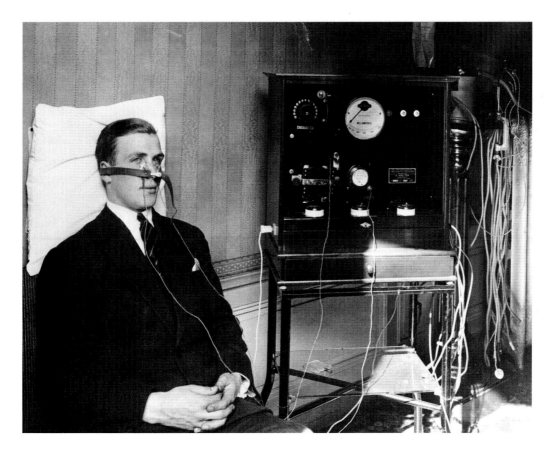

This scientist thought he could cure the common cold by sending electricity into a patient's nose. He was wrong.

strained out all the bacteria in it, then put it in the noses of healthy people—and found that they still got sick.

Many scientists believed that some diseases—including the common cold and influenza—must be caused by viruses. But there was no way to prove their theory before the 1930s, when the electron microscope was invented. This was a newer, much more powerful microscope that allowed scientists to see things far too small to be seen by a regular microscope. For the first time, researchers could actually see viruses, and study their behavior under test conditions.

In 1946, the British government created the Common Cold Unit at Salisbury, near London, England. This was the only research institution in the world dedicated entirely to the study of colds. For decades, volunteers have gone there to be deliberately infected with cold viruses, so that researchers could study their effects. It was scientists at the Common Cold Unit who proved that exposure to cold temperatures and wet conditions did not make anyone more likely to get sick with the common cold.

A researcher at the Common Cold Unit, Sir Christopher Andrewes, identified the first virus known to cause colds, in

A study conducted in 1966 showed how powerful cold-virus infection is. A number of test subjects had the droplets containing the cold virus placed in their noses. Ninety-five percent of them became infected and 75 percent of the infected people got sick. The results of these studies showed scientists just how easy it was to catch a cold.

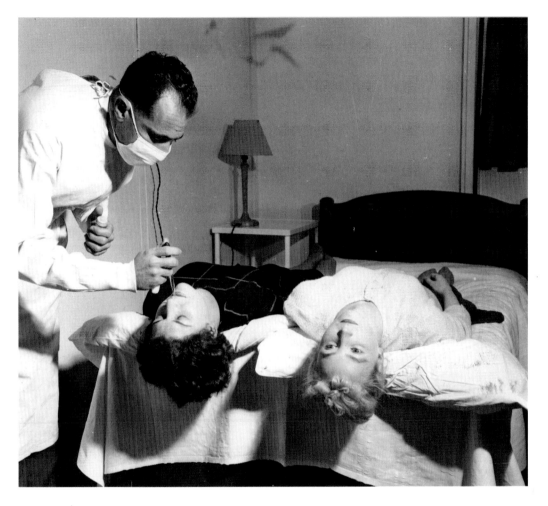

A researcher at the Common Cold Unit in England infects test subjects with cold viruses.

1955. This led many people to predict that a **vaccine** would soon be found to prevent the common cold. But they were wrong.

The common cold has proved to be resistant to cure. One of the most important reasons is that colds are caused not by one virus, but by many. To date, about two hundred viruses known to cause colds have been identified—and many more remain to be found. About one-third of all colds result from viruses that have not yet been identified. Even if all the cold viruses are someday known, it will be very difficult to develop a vaccine that will protect against all of them.

Despite these setbacks, cold research continues all over the world—and sometimes it shows that long-ago remedies actually work. In 1978, for example, Dr. Marvin Sackner of Miami Beach, Florida, conducted an experiment that proved that Maimonides was right. For most people, chicken soup really does make them feel better when they have a cold. It helps to clear away nasal mucus and relieves congestion.

Research has, however, proved that many long-held ideas about colds were wrong. Doctors believed for many years that colds were most often spread by coughing and sneezing. However, it is now clear that the most common method of transmission is by touch.

Scientists are also looking at new approaches to treating—and preventing—the common cold. Many of these approaches focus on finding ways to strengthen the body's immune system. Some people believe, for example, that taking large amounts of vitamin C, zinc (a mineral that occurs naturally in the human body), or an herb called echinacea may reduce the length or severity of a cold. But none of these claims have yet been proved by research. And some of these alternative treatments can bring unpleasant side effects.

There may be other, more effective ways of working with the

Dr. Albert Szent-Gyorgi, a Hungarian-born biochemist, discovered vitamin C, which may help the body fight off the common cold.

These purple cornflowers (left) produce a substance called echinacea. Some people believe echinacea can strengthen the immune system. Echinacea is often sold in pill form (right).

immune system. For example, researchers have conducted experiments on artificially created interferons. A 1986 study showed that people who used a nasal spray containing these interferons had 30 to 40 percent fewer colds. Many more tests will have to be conducted before researchers can be sure that interferon is a safe, effective preventive against colds, but this approach shows real promise.

Another interesting method of fighting colds is through the use of monoclonal antibodies. These are artificial versions of the same antibodies that the human body produces to block viral attacks. This approach, too, shows promise—but it could

These laboratory flasks contain artificially created interferons—substances that someday may help prevent the common cold.

be years before monoclonial antibodies could be used in real-world medical treatment.

Presently, a cure for the common cold has not been found. But the knowledge gained from scientists, doctors, and their patients, has helped the fight against these viruses. Medical professionals may not be able to cure a patient's cold, but they have found ways to help people cope.

4

COPING WITH THE COMMON COLD

It is impossible to avoid getting colds altogether. Almost everyone catches a cold regularly. Even so, there are some things we can do to help protect ourselves against infection by the cold viruses.

LIMITING YOUR EXPOSURE

One of the best ways to avoid catching a cold is to avoid exposure to cold germs from people who are already sick. This is not always easy, of course. Sometimes the people around you may be infected without knowing it, because they have no symptoms. And it is unreasonable to avoid going into public places simply because some people might have colds. But if you can avoid infected people—especially those who are showing early cold symptoms, such as coughing, sneezing, and runny noses—try to do so. This is especially important for babies, who should not be taken out in crowded areas during the first few months of their lives. But if you have to be around people who might have colds, you can do some things that will help you stay cold-free.

Nobody can avoid colds completely. But there are things we can do to help keep them from spreading.

KEEP YOUR HANDS CLEAN

The National Center for Infectious Diseases says, "The most important thing you can do to keep from getting sick is to wash your hands." This is because touch is now widely considered to be the most common method of catching colds. Keeping your hands clean can also prevent you from getting many other, more serious infectious diseases.

You should wash your hands before and after preparing food or eating, after using the bathroom, and after handling animals. And you should also make sure you wash your hands even more

Washing Your Hands

This is the best way to wash your hands: Get your hands wet and then apply soap (bar or liquid) all over your hands. Rub your hands together (making sure you rub all across the surfaces of your hands) for ten to fifteen seconds. Rinse your hands-make sure all the soap is gone— and then dry them well.

By washing your hands regularly—using plenty of soap and rinsing well—you can reduce your chances of getting sick.

often when someone in your family is sick. When you are around people who have colds or are sick, try not to touch your face, your mouth, or your nose until after you have washed your hands.

PRACTICE A HEALTHY LIFESTYLE

Many people believe that a healthy lifestyle can strengthen the immune system, which in turn will increase resistance to infections. This is not yet entirely supported by research, however. But it is certainly a good idea to maintain your general health. This includes getting plenty of rest, exercising regularly, and eating a nutritious and balanced diet.

A well-balanced diet, with lots of fruit and vegetables, can help you stay healthy during cold season.

It is also important to avoid harmful personal habits such as smoking. Besides causing other illnesses, smoking can make cold symptoms worse. This is because smoking affects a person's breathing and having a cold can make breathing even more difficult.

WHAT DO YOU DO IF YOU CATCH A COLD?

No matter how careful you are, the reality is that sooner or later, you are probably going to get a cold. Studies suggest that you will probably have between fifty and one hundred colds in your lifetime. So it is a good idea to know what to do when it happens.

Get Plenty of Rest. All the experts agree: One of the most important things you can do when you have a cold is to get plenty of rest. Fighting a cold is hard work for your body. Your body becomes very tired and needs more energy to function properly. It also needs to have enough energy to continue fighting the virus. Resting and taking it easy helps your body to save energy and use this energy properly. You do not necessarily have to stay in bed all the time, but you should definitely get as much rest as is reasonable.

Drink Fluids. When you have a cold—and especially when you have a fever—you lose a great deal of the fluid in your body. It is absolutely essential that you replace this liquid. If you do not, your risk of contracting serious complications, such as bronchitis and pneumonia, increases greatly.

You can replace a lot of the liquid in your body by drinking eight ounces or more of liquids every two hours. Some liquids work better than others. Fruit juices and—as Maimonides told us, almost a thousand years ago—chicken soup can loosen mucus, make your sore throat feel better, and replace the water your body has lost. Milk usually does not help, because it can create more mucus.

Keep Warm. When you have chills—one of the signs that your immune system is fighting an infection—make sure you keep warm, by wearing a sweater or covering yourself with a thin blanket. If you feel warm, a cool, damp cloth on your forehead might help you feel better.

Clear Out the Mucus. Blowing your noise and coughing help clear your nasal passages, throat, and chest. Your body is trying to

Drinking fluids, such as orange juice, may help keep a cold from getting worse.

get the germ-filled mucus out of your body. You can help it along by gently blowing your nose and coughing. If your nose feels very stuffy or is running a lot, it is okay to gently blow it

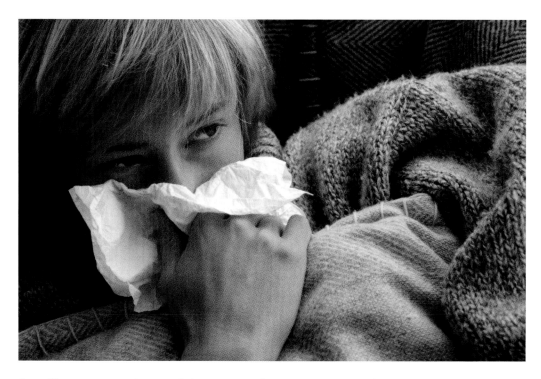

A stuffy, runny nose is one of the most unpleasant symptoms of a cold. But it is also a sign that the body is fighting the infection.

into a tissue. But do not blow too hard or too often, since you can hurt yourself. Coughing can also help to loosen mucus in your throat or chest. Whether coughing or blowing your nose, be sure to wash your hands well afterward.

Some experts suggest warm showers may help. Many think that the steam from the warm water can help to loosen the mucus in the nose, throat, and chest. But be very careful not to make the water too hot. Also, if you are feeling lightheaded and dizzy, make sure you have an adult help you in the bath or the shower—you do not want to fall and hurt yourself.

MEDICATION

It is important to remember that medication cannot cure a cold. They can only help to reduce the symptoms of a cold—and only for a short time. Many doctors believe that it is usually best not to take any kind of medication for a cold. And if you do take cold medicine, you should be very careful. Mixing cold medication or taking too much of one kind can cause serious health problems. Read the labels carefully. You need to make sure you are not taking the same medication in more than one form. Many medications use the same ingredients, and it is easy to take too much. Children should never take any kind of medication, for any reason, unless an adult says it is all right.

There are three main types of medicines that are used to treat the symptoms of the common cold.

Pain medications. Acetaminophen can help reduce headaches and body aches, and

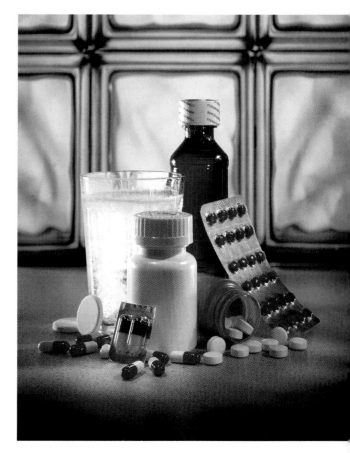

Medication like these can help ease the symptoms of the common cold, at least for a while. But, like all medication, they should be used very carefully.

is also an effective fever-reducer. Many people use aspirin for regular headaches or body aches, but aspirin should ***never*** be taken when you have a cold or other virus-based illness. Experts believe that children and infants who take aspirin at those times can develop a serious disease called Reye's syndrome.

Decongestants. Decongestants are used to decongest—or clear up—your airways. Most decongestants work by shrinking the swollen tissues in your nose. This clears away nasal congestion,

Warning

....

Some medications are thought to be ineffective or inappropriate for people who have colds. Antihistamines—a type of drugs used to treat an **allergy**—are not an effective cold fighter. They may, in fact, lower the body's resistance to disease.

Antibiotics are a type of medicine that fight infections caused by bacteria or other types of germs. They do not fight viruses. A doctor might prescribe antibiotics if there is a serious non-virus infection that is a result of your cold. (Pneumonia or bronchitis are two examples.) But most doctors should not prescribe antibiotics if you have a simple cold. The antibiotics cannot cure the cold. Taking antibiotics for virus infections can actually be very dangerous. Antibiotic resistance has become a huge health problem.

This is a result of people taking antibiotics when they do not need them. Many types of illnesses have become very bad and very strong because some antibiotics no longer work to treat them. This is why it is very important for patients—and their doctors—to be careful about taking and prescribing medicine.

Alternative treatments are often used by people who have colds. These might include pills or teas made of special herbs, flowers, or plants. Echinacea is one example. Some people claim that these substances make their colds go away faster or reduce the strength of the cold symptoms. Doctors and scientists do not know for sure if these claims are true. Taking herbs or plants that are not regulated by the government's strict drug standards—as some of these herbs are not—can be dangerous. Alternative treatments may cause unexpected health problems or may interact dangerously with other medication.

and temporarily makes it easier for you to breathe. Decongestants are available over-the-counter in pill form and as nasal sprays. (Some nasal sprays are actually made of salt and water.) There are also very strong decongestants that a doctor can prescribe if he or she thinks you really need them. However, decongestants can have unpleasant side effects. Some decongestants can make you feel

Many people believe that certain herbs can help fight illness. These herbs are often made into tea.

sleepy or dizzy. They can also sometimes make it hard for you to sleep. In some people, decongestants make their hearts beat too fast, which can be very dangerous. As with most medicine, it is very important to be careful when taking decongestants. In many cases, you should not take decongestants if you are taking other types of medicine of other illnesses.

Cough Medication. Cough medication can be purchased in pill form, or as a syrup that you can drink. Some cough medicines work by affecting the part of the brain that causes you to cough. Others reduce coughing by shrinking the swollen tissues in your throat. This in turn limits the amount of mucus that is produced. But both types of cough medication cause

Cough medication is often taken in a flavored syrup. This makes it taste better, and also helps ease a sore throat.

side effects, including drowsiness.

Cough drops that you suck on are sometimes called lozenges. Different types of lozenges can work in different ways. Some are used to ease or numb sore throats. Others are used to help loosen mucus in your airways. When you choosing a cough drop, have an adult help you read the labels. Certain ingredients in cough drops might cause some people to have a bad reaction—for example their skin might get itchy and swollen, or they may have problems breathing. Also, many cough drops sometimes have a lot of sugar, which can be bad for some people with special health problems. You should never eat a cough drop when you are lying down—you might choke. Taking a cough drop can also be dangerous if you are coughing a lot. Coughing a lot may increase your chances of inhaling, swallowing, or choking on the lozenge.

WHEN SHOULD YOU SEE A DOCTOR?

The common cold sometimes requires medical treatment. You should contact your doctor if you do not feel a lot better after a week, or if you have especially severe—serious—symptoms, including high fever, trouble breathing, or chest pains.

Some people should see a doctor any time they have a cold. These people include children under ten years of age (especially babies), people over seventy, women who are pregnant, and people who have certain **chronic** medical conditions, such as asthma and severe allergies. People who have weak immune systems also need to see a doctor if they catch a cold.

One of the most important reasons to see a doctor under these circumstances is that the common cold can lead to—

If you have a bad cold that lasts more than a week, you should probably be examined by a doctor.

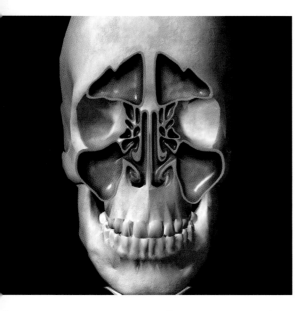

The sinus cavities (shown here in red) often fill up with mucus during a cold. This sometimes leads to painful sinus infections.

or mask the symptoms of—more serious illnesses. Sometimes the viral infection that causes the common cold spreads beyond the areas of the nose and throat. When this happens, it can lead to a number of much more serious conditions. These conditions may include ear infections, which are especially common in children. In an ear infection, the parts and tissues inside the ear become irritated and painful. Sometimes doctors will prescribe medication to treat the ear infections.

Sinus infections are another problem that can develop from colds. The human head has several cavities—or pockets of space—called sinuses. Sinus infections often cause headaches, pressure, and pain. A doctor usually treats a sinus with medication.

One particularly serious cold-related illness is bronchitis. The bronchi (each of these bronchi is called a bronchus) are parts of the lungs. Air passes through them when you breathe. Bronchitis is the inflammation of the bronchi. This illness causes a long-lasting cough, wheezing (a whistling sound during breathing), and sometimes a fever. This condition can cause serious damage to the lungs, and it should always be treated by a doctor.

Another cold complication is pneumonia. It can be caused by either a virus or bacteria, and can cause severe coughing, chest pain, extreme chills, and fevers as high as 105 degrees Fahrenheit. Pneumonia can be extremely serious—the high fevers associated with it can actually cause brain damage and it can even cause death. Like bronchitis, pneumonia should always be treated by a doctor.

Pinkeye

A common illness among people of all ages is conjunctivitis—also known as pinkeye. Conjunctivitis affects a part of your eyes called the conjunctiva. When you have pinkeye, your eyes become teary, red, and itchy and they may secrete—push out—goopy or crusty substances called discharge. Doctors sometimes prescribe medicine to treat pinkeye.

Conjunctivitis can be a result of allergies or it can be caused by an infection. Scientists do not know why, but many people seem more likely to catch conjunctivitis during or after having a cold. This could have something to do with a weakened immune system, or it could also be a result of cold germs somehow infecting the eyes. Whatever the reason, when you have a cold you should try to avoid touching or rubbing your eyes. (Even when you are healthy you should be careful about touching your eyes.) Also, you should never touch your eyes—or the area near your eyes—with tissue paper that you have used to wipe or blow your nose. If you have to wipe or clean your eyes, make sure you have clean hands and use clean tissue paper or a washcloth.

When you have a cold, rubbing may make your tired, itchy eyes feel a little better, but it can also spread your infection.

A cough is a familiar symptom of the common cold. But it can also be a sign of other, more serious illnesses.

People who have asthma need to be especially careful when they have colds. Having asthma sometimes makes it very difficult to breathe, and the mucus in the lungs can increase this problem. People who begin wheezing during a cold should see a doctor.

WHEN IS A COLD NOT A COLD?

Another reason to go to a doctor is that sometimes what seems to be a cold is really something else— sometimes something much more serious. Influenza—called the flu for short—is an example. Flu symptoms are often like cold symptoms. The symptoms of the flu include fever (this is a more common symptom than with the common cold), coughing, body aches, and malaise. One important difference is that colds usually appear slowly, while influenza seems to strike quickly. Only a doctor can determine whether you have the flu.

Other illnesses and medical conditions can easily be mistaken for the common cold, too. These include allergies—which can cause many of the same symptoms as colds, such as coughing,

The Cost of the Common Cold

The National Center for Health Statistics estimates that every year, 62 million colds are serious enough to make people seek medical attention or restrict—limit—their activities. For example, colds often make many people stay home from work or school.

A recent study by the University of Michigan Health System shows that all those colds have a huge financial effect. This study estimated that the common cold cost the United States economy billions of dollars every year. More than 100 million doctor visits every year were caused by colds. The total cost of these visits is estimated to be around $7.7 billion. Another $400 million was spent on cold medications prescribed—ordered—by doctors. About $2.9 billion was spent on unprescribed over-the-counter cold remedies.

The effects of the cold common cold can cost a lot of money in other ways. For example, on February 27, 1969, the National Aeronautics and Space Administration (NASA) had to delay the Apollo 9 space mission, because all three of the astronauts had colds. Delaying the launch cost NASA more than half a million dollars.

cause many of the same symptoms as colds, such as coughing, sneezing, sore throats, and runny noses—and many serious childhood illnesses, such as chicken pox, measles, and mumps.

THE FUTURE OF THE COMMON COLD

Despite many medical and technological advances and everything we know about the cold, we still do not have a cure for it. The common cold is proving to be one of the most stubborn diseases medical sciences has ever faced. We know far more about colds than we did even a few years ago. But we also know one thing for certain: The common cold will still be with us for a long, long time.

GLOSSARY

airways—The passages in the throat and nose that allow air to travel to and from the lungs.

allergy—An extreme sensitivity to foreign substances, such as certain foods, pollen, animal hair, or dust.

antibiotic—A type of medication that can cure some diseases caused by bacteria and some other microorganisms.

antibody—A substance that white blood cells create to defend against microorganisms that can cause disease.

asthma—A disease of the respiratory system that causes wheezing, coughing, and shortness of breath.

bacteria—A group of microorganisms (separate from viruses), many of which cause diseases.

bronchitis—An inflammation of the passages that carry air to the lungs.

chronic—A disease or other medical condition (such as a disease) that lasts for a long time or happens again and again.

cilia—Small extensions from cells, like tiny hairs, that can block foreign substances from entering some parts of the body.

congestion—An excessive buildup of fluids in some parts of the body, such as mucus in the nose and the throat of someone who has a cold.

contagious—Capable of being spread through contact, or infected with a disease that can be spread.

decongestant—A type of medication that reduces congestion, especially in the nose and sinuses.

fatigue—Tiredness or exhaustion, sometimes caused by illness.

germ—A microorganism, especially one that can cause disease.

histamine—A chemical that is produced by the body in response to an injury or the presence of foreign matter.

host—A cell or organism that is taken over by a parasite, such as a virus.

immunity—The body's ability to resist a disease caused by a foreign substance.

immunoglobulins—Protein substances produced by the immune system. Antibodies are made from immunoglobulins.

incubation period—The time or interval between exposure to an infection and the appearance of the first symptoms.

infection—An invasion of the tissue of an animal or a plant by a microorganism, such as a bacteria or a virus.

interferons—A group of virus-fighting chemicals that are produced naturally by the body.

interleukins—Substances produced by white blood cells in response to infection.

lymphocyte—A type of white blood cell that helps to fight infections.

malaise—A vague feeling of being unwell.

microorganism—A tiny organism so small that it can be seen only with a microscope.

monocyte—A type of white blood cell that helps to fight infection.

mucus—An oily protective substance produced by the mucous membranes.

neutrophil—A type of white blood cell, that help to fight infection.

over-the-counter remedies—Medication that can be purchased without an official prescription from a doctor or healthcare professional.

parasite—An organism, such as a virus, that lives or reproduces by feeding off another organism, called the host.

phlegm—Thick mucus produced in large amounts by the mucus membranes of the respiratory system during a cold or other illness.

pneumonia—An infection of the lungs, caused by either viruses or bacteria.

prostaglandins—Infection-fighting chemicals produced by cells in response to a virus attack.

respiratory system—The parts of the body (including the nose, mouth, throat, and lungs) that are used for breathing.

sinus—One of a group of air-filled cavities in the head.

symptom—Any change in the body that signals the presence of an illness.

vaccine—A type of medication that can prevent infection.

virus—A microorganism that causes many diseases in humans, animals, and plants.

white blood cells—Special blood cells that help protect the body against infection. There are several different types of white blood cells.

FIND OUT MORE

Books

Aaseng, Nathan. *The Common Cold and the Flu*. New York: Franklin Watts, 1992.

Almonte, Paul, and Theresa Desmond. *The Immune System*. New York: Maxwell Macmillan International, 1991.

Benziger, John, and Mary Benziger. *The Corpuscles Meet the Virus Invaders: Fun and Facts about the Common Cold and the Body's Immune System*. Waterville, ME: Corpuscles InterGalactica, 1990.

Birch, Beverly, and Fiona MacDonald. *Louis Pasteur: Father of Modern Medicine*. Woodbridge, CT: Blackbirch Press, 2001.

Kittredge, Mary. *The Common Cold*. Philadelphia: Chelsea House Publishers, 2001.

Morgan, Sally. *Germ Killers: Fighting Disease*. Chicago: Heinemann Library, 2002.

Silverstein, Alvin, Virginia Silverstein, and Laura Silverstein Nunn. *Common Colds*. New York: Franklin Watts, 1999.

Web Sites

Beat the Winter Bugs: How to Hold Your Own against Cold
and Flu
http://www.fda.gov/fdac/features/2001/601_flu.html

Chilling Out with Colds
http://www.kidshealth.org/kid/ill_injure/sick/colds.html

The Common Cold Fact Sheet from the National Institute of
Allergy and Infectious Disease
http://www.niaid.nih.gov/factsheets/cold.htm

Common Cold
http://www.commoncold.org/index.htm

Stalking the Mysterious Microbe (American Society for
Microbiology)
http://www.microbe.org/index.html

Upper Respiratory Infection (Lucile Packard Children's Hospital
at Stanford)
http://www.lpch.org/DiseaseHealthInfo/HealthLibrary/respire/
uricold.html

INDEX

Page numbers for illustrations are in **boldface**

acetaminophen, 9
adults (and colds), 12
allergies, 50, 56, 57
antibiotics, 50
antibodies, 20, 40, 41
aspirin, 34, 50
asthma, 8, 53, 56

bacteria, 29, 30, 35, 55
body aches, 10, 49, 50
breathing, 8, 46, 53
bronchitis, 10, 46, 50, 54-55

"catching a cold" *See* contagiousness
chicken soup, 9, 27, **34,** 38, 47
children (and colds), 11, 12, **12,** 25, **25,** 42, 43, **43**
chills, 7, 10, 47, 56
cilia, 19, **19**
cold season, 18
complications, 17, 46, 53, 56
congestion, 7, 15, 24
conjunctivitis *See* pinkeye
contagiousness, 8, 11, 12, 17, **17,** 18, 25, 35, 36, 37, **37,** 42, 44-45
   See also exposure
coronavirus, 14, **14**
cough, 7, 9, 10, 15, 17, 19, 25, **25,** 42, 47, 51, 56, 57
cure, 9, 13, 26-28, **27**

decongestants, 50, 51
diet, 45
drinking, 9, 46-47, **47**
duration of cold, 10
ears, 54

echinacea, 38, 40, **40,** 41, 50
ephedrine, 26
exposure, 17, **17,** 18
eyes, 55
   See also pinkeye

fatigue, 7
fever, 6, 7, 10, 15, 22, 25, 50, 53, 55
flu, 10, 35, 56
fluids, 9

germ theory, 29
germs, 18, 42, 55

hand washing, 44, **44,** 45
headache, 6, 9, 25
herbs, 38, 40, 50, 51
histamine, 20-21
history, 26-41, **27, 29, 31, 32, 33, 34, 35, 37, 39, 40, 41**
host, 14, 16, **16,** 20
hygiene, 44, **44**

immune system, 11, 12, 20-25, **21,** 36, 37, 38, 45
immunity, 11, 20-21
immunoglobulins, 20
incubation period, 25
infection, 10, 11, 18, 20, 21, 42
influenza, *See* flu
interferons, 22, 38, 40, 41, **41**
interleukin, 22

lungs, 10, **11,** 54, 55
lymphocytes, 21-22

malaise, 7, 15, 25, 56
medication, 6, 9, 30-34, **32, 33,** 49-53, **49, 51, 52,** 57
   cough drops, 52
   cough syrup, **49,** 51, 52, **52**
   over-the-counter, 51, 57

pain, 50
See also antibiotics, aspirin, decongestants

monocyte, 21-22
mouth, **11,** 17, **17, 45**
mucus, 7, 17, **17,** 18, 19, 20, 21, 22, **24,** 25, 35, 47, 48
muscle aches, 20, 21, 22

neutrophil, 20, 21, **21**
nose, **11,** 17, **17,** 18, 18-19, 20, 22, **24,** 35, 42, 44, 45, 47, 48
  blowing, 47, 48, **48**

parasite, 14
  See also virus
pinkeye, 55
pneumonia, 10, 46, 50, 55
prevention (of colds), 12, 42
prostaglandins, 20
proteins, 20

research, 28-41, **29, 31, 35, 37**
respiratory syncytial virus (RSV), 15, **15**
respiratory system, 10, 11, **11**
rest, 9, 45, 46
Reye's syndrome, 50
rhinovirus, 15, **15,** 23, **23**

sinus, 26, 54, **54**
  infection, 54
sneezing, 7, 9, 10, 15, 17, **17,** 25, 27, 28, 42, 57

statistics, 10, 11, 12, 18, 36, 37, 57
swelling, 20, 21, 51
symptoms, 6-9, 10, 42, 46
  See also chills, cough, fever, headache, malaise, sneezing, throat soreness

temperature, 6-7, 25
throat, 10, 11, **11,** 22, **24,** 48, 52
  soreness, 6, 9, 10, 15, 21, 22, 52, 57
tissue, 18, 51, 54
treatment, 8, 9, 10, 13, 20-21, 22, 25, 26-28, **27,** 36, 37, 38, 46-56

vaccine, 36, 37
virus, 10, 13, **13,** 15, 16, 18, 19, 20-25, 35, 36, 37
  discovery of, 30, **31**
  reproduction, 14, 16, **16,** 22, 23, **23**
  types of cold, 14, **14,** 15, **15,** 17, 37
  See also coronavirus, respiratory syncytial virus, and rhinovirus
vitamins, 38, **39**
  vitamin C, 38

Web sites, 62
white blood cells, 21, **21**
  See also lymphocytes, monocytes, neutrophils

ABOUT THE AUTHOR

Terry Allan Hicks has written books for Marshall Cavendish about subjects ranging from the Declaration of Independence to the state of Nevada. He lives in Connecticut with his wife, Nancy, and their sons Jamie, Jack, and Andrew. Right this minute, one of them probably has a cold.